# Taxidancing

Also by PAUL PINES

POETRY

*Onion*
*Hotel Madden Poems*
*Pines Songs*
*Breath*
*Adrift on Blinding Light*

PROSE

*The Tin Angel*
*Redemption*
*My Brother's Madness*

# Taxidancing

## Paul Pines

*Introduction by*
*Laurel Blossom*

*Collages by*
*Wayne Atherton*

To Barbara —
w pose work I
love —
6.8.08

**IKON**
New York, New York

# Acknowledgments

Acknowledgments: Some of these poems have appeared in *Café Review, House Organ, Alcatraz, The World, Tribes* and on line on *Poetry Bay, Light & Dust Books* and *Tamafyhr Mountain Poetry.* For publication online I am grateful to Rochelle Ratner, George Wallace, Carl Young, and Kenneth Gurney. My gratitude, too, to Susan Sherman for her continued support, to Wayne Atherton for his inspired images and to Laurel Blossom for her intelligent reading of this book. Finally, I'd like to thank the Tribeca Performing Arts Center for honoring the Tin Palace in its series of Lost Jazz Shrines.

Photo Credit for the back cover: Carol Pines

Library of Congress Control Number: 2007900114
First Edition
Printed in Canada by AGMV Marquis

State of the Arts

**NYSCA**

This publication is made possible with public funds from the New York State Council on the Arts, a State Agency.

IKON
151 First Ave. #46
New York, NY 10003
ikoninc@aol.com

# Table of Contents

Bits & Pieces

# Introduction

RENDERED POETRY

The question is: how to pull together a unified point of view concerning the latest book of poetry by Paul Pines - a volume that consists of two sections of distinctly different tone and focus- and, at the same time, to pay due attention to the relationship between individual fragments and the whole?

Perhaps the answer is in a short passage by the author in his poem "The Whirlwind: After Sonny Rollins." In the poem, Pines defines the verb "to render,//that is, to interpret/and tear apart//simultaneously."

It is this oppositional strategy, as applied by the author that binds two disparate sections of Taxidancing, Paul Pines's sixth book of poetry.

In the first section "After Hours," the author reflects on the period when he lived on the Lower East Side of New York City, supporting himself as a taxi driver, bar keeper, and jazz club owner. The poems visually jump on the page, their rhythms are hopped up, and the vignettes described are full of poets, jazzmen, acquaintances, neighborhood joints and local color. They succeed in evoking the 1970s New York scene without sentimentality, but with a familiarity that embraces the reader.

"Adios Pablo," for instance, begins: "Once he told me//I'm trying to enter/my 44th year/with a little dignity//tipping his Stetson/with his thumb/and sat//(you know/the way he used/to...)" Pines tells his stories straight and spare. His attitude is amused and amusing, detached and, at the same time, tender with human compassion.

By contrast, the second section, "Bits And Pieces," seems at first discontinuous with the first. It delves into fragments of religious, artistic, and political philosophy, Christian, Jewish, Muslim, Native American, animistic, and particularly Buddhist, where Pines seems most comfortably to find a home. His spiritual exploration leads him to the eventual conclusion that everything includes everything else, any one passion or desire opens into all aliveness ("every passion/leads us/from a known thing/back/into a deep/unknown"), and all fragments imply a whole, "(even in the uncertainty/that moves us forward/into uncertainty)."

Recapturing the lost may once have seemed his primary artistic mission, but Pines's ideas seem to change as the book proceeds. Sorrow "is also/the source of desire," he says in the poem "Homenaje al Neruda". In accepting this reality, Pines absorbs his, and humanity's, unspecified losses and grows into something greater. He grows "tired of myself in time" ("Pin-headed Angel Dance") and moves towards eternity, from the madness of existential struggle to the "darkness of a dream" in which "each of us [is] a center."

The last poem, "Way of the Warrior," sums up nicely the arc of Pines's spiritual taxi ride. It reads in its entirety:

I planted my madness
in the world

watched it grow
and fade

like a wildflower
on a hillside

*

Wayne Atherton's collages reflect the complex unity of the book, offering contrapuntal rhythm; one of them is even called "Justaposition."The charming cover collage of yellow cabs, Pines's expired taxi driver's license (stepped on by a man's foot), black and white background photos of a period car and what looks like a New York streetscape is the only one that directly refers to the poet or the overt subjects of the poems. Otherwise the collages are more or less wry psychological commentaries, enjoying common elements like black and white images, film strips, bands of plastic mesh, hands, figures, masks, bits of fabric and shards of landscape that seem to become increasingly disturbing as the book progresses.

So it seems that while Atherton's collages grow more disruptive, Pines's poems seem to move in the opposite direction, towards resolution and serenity. Pines writes, "[I] thought it was the details/I wanted to preserve/mistook events/ in themselves/as precious//when it was really/what escaped/me/as I went." ("Kicking Up Dust").

Laurel Blossom

# After Hours

Oh, to be the nameless member of a quartet like I heard today!
— Charles Mingus, Beneath The Underdog

## Taxidancing

Out of the garage
by sunrise
cruising for fares

nothing seems clear
but the meter
which is divine.

We know the bee
is spectacular
among creatures

that its life
is orderly

its law nourishing.

Solomon was told
to study the drone
as I do now

stuck to my seat
at the intersection
of 57th and 3rd...

I think

9 isn't what
it's cracked up to be,
all head and no feet

6 is 9
asleep or in vitro

side by side
they form Cancer
the voluptuous Crab

or a form of sex

in which we struggle for air

the Romans
gave their numbers
a foundation and a roof

which they used until
barbarians became bureaucrats

3 isn't much better
in spite of its publicity
simply an implication

of 8
that sidewinder INFINITY

of which we are reflections
so pale
I want to jump the light!

# The Tin Palace Troll

When TEX ALLEN
leaned across Bradley's bar
to thank me for the years
I let him practice
in my basement

I thought:
> *What's done is done.*
> *The world breeds new joints*
> *and savvy kids*
> *and mornings so long-of-tooth*
> *you wonder they were*
> *ever otherwise.*

"Lissen," he said. "You're a poet
and it musta been tuff
running a club but if you never do anything else
you've done enuf
and if I didn't tell you this
I'd be worth less than a weed
that owes something to the sod."

# Hitler's Favorite Trumpet Player

—For Karl Stuecklen

Eddie Jefferson told me
when Hitler wanted

to hear jazz in Paris
he looked for this guy

we see all the time
on Second Avenue

in a brown silk suit
gold cuff links

and a rug on his head
with peaks

like the Hartz Mountains.
This morning I spot him

hatless in the rain
bent over a mail box

on 5th Street
whispering down a damp

chute:
*"Il ne veut passer!"*

## Jazzmobile

Did you

  dig

     Dexter

dancing

       in front of

         Grant's Tomb

when

  his keyboard

     took a solo?

       HE DID THE LUSITANIA!
*puffing*
   *a cigarette*
    *arched*
     *his back*
      *fanned*
       *his knees*
        *and listed...*
          a ship
          with explosive cargo

# Cocaine Cadenza

After Bradley
finishes his last set
I see his nose
has become

          pitted
          as moon rock

          a surface of craters

          a terrain on which
          bulges grow from
          other bulges
          like Black Forest
          mushrooms

          a huge sponge
          with a
               starboard
                   list

          a creature
          that has started
          to drift
               leaving
             a small
             abyss
          in the middle
          of his face

# After Hours

I love
to be dissolute with you

get high
and stay up all night
      listening
      to jazz

Every time
you move I watch

your breasts
through that sleeveless
      blouse
hear
      your thighs rub
      in harem pants

and feel
the ocean shift...

how could anyone say
I've wasted my life?

# Tompkin Square Meditation

Those yellow leaves,
an immense burden of detail
for such narrow limbs,

remind me of the way
things are turned around
these days

           a spring rain in autumn
the economy in trouble
Laurie back from
the Philippines
by way of
India

      a long time manic
      on the phone

something in her voice
about to give
about to flower
  out of season

         so hard to return
         and live

to be as free at home
as you were
on the other side of the world

# The Whirlwind: After Sonny Rollins

These are possibilities,
currents at the center

of stones. At times
you can feel what

your senses mean:
to render,

that is, to interpret
and tear apart

simultaneously
where the wind is sown

# Meteorology: After Philip Guston

The weatherman
    is born
        not made

a kid rushing out to catch
    the first
            snow
                    flake
a tiny seismograph
    registering
        every change
of light...

In the same way I have
    always been
        a writer
                which is
                why I
                am
        applying for a

    NELSON ALGREN AWARD

and declaring
according to your rules
    that I am in

        financial need:

                if you require
                further proof
                I can send you snapshots
                of my shoes

# The Death of Ted Berrigan

He died
on Independence Day
1983
of a heart attack
carrying too much weight
and cigarette
ashes
in his beard

At his Memorial
in St. Mark's
Sanders likened him
to Blackburn
O'Hara
and Millay
while Padgett
couldn't find words
to describe his friend
of twenty-four years

After Hollo
expressed surprise
Ted beat him to the grave
everyone
paraded
outside
behind
Schneeman's
painting of the poet
naked
in a chair
which moved
a wino
to leap from
the Ottendorfer Library steps
screaming,

*Praise Him!*
*Praise the Lord!*

# Bebop Head: for Richie Cole

What you say
gets lost in
what you said

always hungry
for more than
words can say

and hunger is
what it's about
no matter how

good the ear
soft the voice
slim the body.

How fat was
Eddie J.
Bird or Fats

Navaro? But
the real
question is

what do you
do if you're
still hungry

and don't have
any more time
on your hands.

# Good-Bye Joe: A Eulogy Delivered by Mickey Tucker

When I first got to the City
before I was married
Joe Carroll said,

> *Mickey Tucker*
> *I love my wife, Alma, so much*
> *I wouldn't leave her*
> *to go to heaven.*
>> That was
>> the only time
>> he ever lied to me

# Adios Pablo

—for Paul Blackburn

Once he told me

> *I'm trying to enter*
> *my 44th year*
> *with a little dignity*

tipping his Stetson
with his thumb
and sat

     (you know
       the way he used
        to...)

        head tilted
       back
          cat-eyes
             squinting

       and that fibrous smile
          on his face cracking
            like an egg

# Blues for Dick and Jane

All things are on fire
  even the moon. See
    how it puckers
      around every
        orifice?

We burn at different rates.

Most poets go mad
  or discover
    others fixing dinner
      who will share
        what they
          have
            made

*the conversion of matter into energy*

      our hearts strive for
       at a ratio of 2:1
        but it's
     never as easy as
              Dick & Jane
    or anyone
     loves
       someone...

  it was Spot
    they watched run

      who ran away
        and set them both
          in motion

# Justaposition

# Malcolm's Blues

Should I
  who have
    an assassin
      in my throat
              be dumb
              be gone
              be shy
    lie
      by silence
        and explode
          or let my words
            like lava
              on my tongue
                burn out
                  and fossilize?
Allah!
        I'm burning up
          there are hands
            in my gut
              that catch
                my breath

                should I hide
                  in the shadow
                    of my lungs
                      or
                  find peace
                marking time
        on a ziggurat?

              O, Mecca
                of my distant
                quick
                    *how many ghosts*
                    *in my bones*
                    *how many bones*
                    *in your walls*
                    *how many ways to*
                    *skin them alive*

# Monk's Dream

Twisting
  the symphony
    as Ives
      did

          but
            with
              one
                finger

        a single
        note
    implied

between the keys
    a note
      we can't
        hear


  no less
  look at

      call white
          or black...

# Largo

—for Lisa Bond

Maybe
in the end
it's not the poet
who wins
but the one
who wanted to
be a poet

because
the will is not
a beacon
but a match
struck
in the wind

and all we teach
each other
or are taught
begins
and ends
as soon as it
is thought

and every passion
leads us
from a known thing
back
into a deep
unknown

# The Way It Happened

—for Al Kovacs

The ACADEMY OF AMERICAN POETS
invited me to read
with two other poets in City Hall Park.
It was a cloudy day
and I arrived to find activity
on the steps of City Hall—
a podium facing several rows of folding chairs
adjacent to a brass band
tuning up with a medley from Oklahoma.
It seemed marvelous to find
                      Poetry, Politics
                      and a Broadway Musical
converging on Wall Street
when a lady on the steps said
she was sorry—this wasn't a poetry event
but a ceremony to honor the courageous
   handicapped of New York.
And I watched them
stumbling out of taxis
struggling from the subway like pilgrims
heading for the shrine at St. Anne de Beaupres.

I located my event further south
on a plot of grass surrounded by junkies
and joined the poets
who greeted me like survivors on a rubber raft.
The Academy official was setting up our podium
when a sculptor named Al appeared
with short hair and a crew neck sweater
looking like an Economist who'd been drowned
   by his students in the Liffy.
I hadn't seen him for years
since he'd lost fifty pounds and shaved
a beard that had hung in knots
   like DeBuffet's
               *Beard of Perpetual Sorrow.*

"You know," he told the poets next to me,
"I'm always moved by this part of town.

That building over there,
the one they're washing...yes, that one.
It's very special. My father
committed suicide in it trying to prove
    he could play chess.
That was the last time I saw him."

I noticed that while Al
had cleaned up his body his eyeballs
    seemed to bulge
                    and took him aside
aware others were regarding us
as harbingers of Municipal Confusion.

"What have you been doing?" I asked.

"Oh, you know, walking up and down,
working a lot with the Himalayan She-Goat.
Have you ever been to Peru?
No?
Maybe we can go together.
You can drift on Titicaca in a balsa boat
    while I carve in stone—
which is getting more difficult for me
    at this altitude.
I'm doing it less and less.
It may also be the shape of my head
    or my bones.
I've got to get up high
    or wait until they thicken."

"You've got nice ears," I observed.

"Thanks. Would you like to meet them?
This one, here, is Beethoven.
And this one's Van Gogh."

"Pleased to meet you."

"You've got cute ears yourself," he smiled.

"I'll bet a poet with your ears

could work well in stone.
Would you join me for coffee?"
"Perhaps next year," I told him
as the band for the handicapped
   struck up The Impossible Dream.
"Right now I have to bring poetry
   to the people."

"Well done." Al pumped my hand.

"See you later." I waved.
 "Best of luck in Peru."

# The Radix

—for brother Claude

Fire

    (what the work is)
                         set
against myself:
            that dream
            whose voice pursues.

Everything
is fire but what conducts fire:

            *Wake up!* it says.

# Artifacts

—for William Bronk

The house on Pearl Street is as it was
 in gothic disarray
                    Loren's iron scuplture
                    (a lance stuck through a shield)
                    sits on the porch
bare ginkos
in the December afternoon
hover over the dormers like dowagers
over a tombstone
                    I enter
through the kitchen
a half-eaten apple on the table
beside your inhalers the compressor
a potentate by the telephone
bellowing orders to an empty sun porch
I follow the hose into the front room
where you lie hooked at the nose
to the other end
                    under a threadbare
                    red comforter
stretched out on the couch
your head high-domed
beneath a fringe
of white hair
hugging yourself
restless blue-nailed fingers
at your chest work
to fill your lungs
with air
knit unspoken
words
            I sit on the window seat
            and wait
not for you
to wake
            but something
            else...
all the old artifacts
are here
            Canaday's darkly etched

36

                    variations on
                    the Chambered
                    Nautilus
Marril's
Provincetown seascapes
Peter's ingenious
mobile
                    sunbeams
                    on the Persian rugs

winter light fills the room .

                    (as it always does
                    as it never will
                    again)

I feel it in my bones

there is an end
to learning
                    its aquisition
                    and utility
and to
love

# So Long

*O thicker and faster—(So long!)*
*O crowding too close upon me..*
— Walt Whitman

So Long
means
            Good-bye or
            It's been so
            long since I've
            seen you or
            will be so long before we
            meet again or the suggestion
            of unspecified duration so

Sal was spreading mayonnaise
on the mortadella
while a young Puerto Rican
stared at the knife
and sang:
            *Make it nice*
            *Make it nice*
            *Put a little more*
            *meat on that bread*

and we laughed
because an April sun was turning
everything in the Deli
liquid gold and
we were warm
after a cold winter
my 39th

then Sal
buttered me a roll
poured a coffee to go
and put them in a bag
as the light struck me
like the slap of
a Zen Roshi

and I realized
it would be easier

than I had thought
to enter my 40's
with a little
dignity
regardless
of my
circumstances
so I told Sal

      *So long, Sal,*
      *so long*

# Bits and Pieces

I reflected that even in the languages
of humans there is no proposition
that does not imply the entire universe...

—Joge Luis Borges, *The Writing Of The God*

## books are...the *children of silence.*

— Proust

to be a fisher of memory
is not the same as being a fisher of men

to be a fisher of men
one must know everything

synchronously
never cleaving to a single historical detail

to be a fisher of one's own heart
is to share assumptions with no one

to bait a sensation and reel up
a century in silence

# The Persistence of Memory

The smoke of your fire
still smolders
in the eaves of Rouen
Jean D'Arc
        my soul
        in ashes

# We Build Our Shrines Where We Once Refused to Go

—for David Unger

I was taught to recite
the 23rd Psalm at bed time
before entering
a wilderness
                that left me
                scared
late into the night

Calling out
to a father
            who would not
            comfort me
I wondered at
the assurance David
wrung from fear
                a boy so small
                a sling shot
                of a boy
                like me

who understood
that shadows
form
            an underground
            stream

on which he
had been set
adrift

# The Secret Doctrine

—for Dalt Wonk

the Bal Shem Tov
suggests
the sight of a single soul
in the after world
renders
all argument
moot

# Squirrels

A generation of squirrels
is killing itself

because of the extended
summer drought there is

something untoward
in the seasonal patterns

parents have become
neglectful or defunct

leaving their children
unprepared for the world

nothing can be done
to compensate

for this lack of adult
guidance and tiny corpses

litter the highway
where they've tried to cross

unable to judge when
to go forward

or retreat mouths full
of nuts and old corn cobs

these little pieces of nature
with a death wish

# Ansel Acid

*the Vedas is now revealed to thee*

— Sankara

Monsters
are born
            in the dark
            and come
            to light

they exist
to show you
            the shape
            of your
            fear

which you
begin to see
            is the door
            to your
            heart

that you have
located
            in despair
            but enter
            in
sadness...

            a wave
                        that carries you
                        away from old
                        wounds

48

# Kicking Up dust

Duke at bat
Jackie stealing home

from Flatbush
to lower East Side 60s
push carts in autumn
on Avenue C

       heatless winter
       bed-bug nights
       snow like lace
       on fire escapes
the track in my father's head
where they drilled for cancer
       Hank Moble
       and Ornette
       at Sluggs

acid rain
of bodies falling past
my window
       on 6th & Boo
LSD Magi who thought
they could fly

       finally shipping out
          spring on tramps
          Gulfwise summers
          December on
          the North Atlantic

United Fruit banana boat
to Olangapo
and Nam
          bamboo roofs
          ablaze
          New Year's Eve
          Tu Do Street
          Saigon 1965

returned with malarial fevers

mouth
and head
on fire

      to convalesce
      in Yucatan
      among Mayans
      from Chic-Xulub
      outside Progresso...

            thought it was the details
            I wanted to preserve
            mistook events
            in themselves
            as precious
                  when it was really
                  what escaped
                  me
                  as I went

# I am that Brahman which is like space

— Sankara

*The Crest Jewel of Wisdom* suggests
my psyche interfaces with the universe

(Brahman and I
linked by a darkness that dissolves
all boundaries)
      the black hole
      I will sink
      into
      at death

           is
           a pin point

      at the center
      of the milky way

           that anchors
           the galaxy

# Pin-Headed Angel Dance

—for Fred Waitzkin

Driving home
on Quaker Road

      corn fields gone yellow
      burning bushes everywhere

    I grow old
    as I knew
    I would
        spent my life
        practicing for it
the question that burns
like autumn air
in my lungs
      as Buddha
      stated it
        "what happens
        to a fire
        that's gone out"

what happens
after the dance of leaves
what happens to exploding stars
or salt abandoned by
the sea
      wherewith
      the burning ash
I've
grown
tired of myself in time
and of a universe
in which
     light
     stretched thin
     becomes invisible to
     the eye
        clings
          even
          as it moves
          awayfrom
            its origin

***I have brought thee the Eye of Horus,***
***that thou may equip with it thy face...***

What is the touch of delight
but the seeing hand

in the palm an open eye
that looks out from a place beyond death

we thirst for that clear stream to which
we may draw close but never drink

not even touch the water with our lips
always a membrane between

the eyeless palms of our yearning
the sorrow that separates us

# Anima

The curse you bear
                is your own weight
                I am not she
                All soul is not bent upon
                your undoing

Apart from yourself I am what
                you seek
                I am your heartbeat
                I was always there
                and will be

You need not call me anything
                Where no boundary exists
                between mind and space
                there is no power
                in a name

# Hoops

Everything wants to be a circle.
— Black Elk Speaks

Black Elk spoke
of the hoop
>              a flowering tree
>              roots & branches
>              extending into upper
>              and lower
>              worlds
at the center
where time and eternity
meet
>        and overflow
>                        a hoop of abundance
>                        enclosing
>                        the hoop
>                                    of each person
>                                    inside the hoop of each nation
>                                    inside the hoop of the planet
>                        like ripples in a floating universe


the hoop of the mind
expanding within those others
>                              each of us
>                              a center
>                              corresponding
>                              to centers
that open
into the darkness of a dream
in which I hear his voice
see a sand painting of the tree
restored
>              yellow and red leaves
>              reaching into my world
>              the autumnal splendor
>              of his failed vision

# Baggage

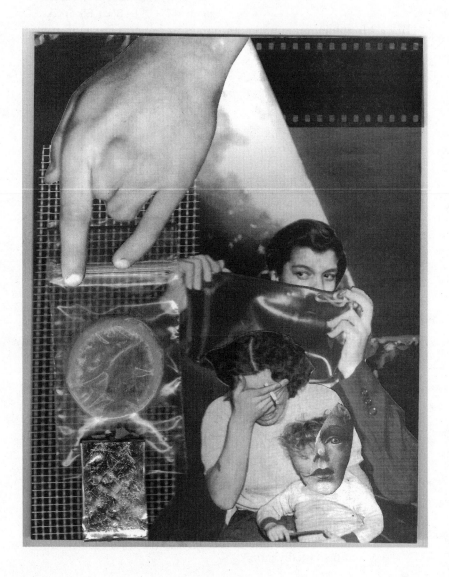

# Homenaje al Neruda

—for Herman Galilea

The interior
is an Arucanian tree
roots pushing into earth
in search of that
sorrow
      which is also
      the source of desire.

There are no politics
apart from this.

What blossoms from it
turns us into lovers
with the hearts
of tigers
      (even in old clothes
       even with gray hair
even in the uncertainty
that moves us forward
into uncertainty)
          there is only this left
          after everything else
          falls away
she who waits
apart from ourselves
that part of
ourselves
      we have missed
      without realizing it
she who has searched for us
where we can't
be found
      and finding us
      wraps us in her shawl
and sings
with the voice of our voice
a lullabye
      in which a fledgling
      rawness beats its wings

# Way of the Warrior

I planted my madness
in the world

watched it grow
    and fade
            like a wildflower
            on a hillside...

**PAUL PINES** grew up in Brooklyn around the corner from Ebbetts Field and passed the early 60s on the Lower East Side of New York. He shipped out as a merchant seaman, spending 65-66 in Vietnam, after which he supported himself driving a taxi and tending bar until he opened his own jazz club, The Tin Palace in 1970 on the corner of 2nd Street and Bowery. A cultural watering hole for the better part of the 70s, it provided the setting for his first novel, The Tin Angel (Wm Morrow, 1983). Pines lived and traveled in Central America through the 80s. The genocidal policy targeting Guatemalan Mayans became the basis for his second novel, Redemption (Editions Rocher, 1997). Curbstone Press will publish his memoir, My Brother's Madness, in fall, 07. Pines has published five books of poetry: Onion, Hotel Madden Poems, Pines Songs, Breath, and Adrift On Blinding Light. Selections set to music by composer Daniel Asia appear on *Songs From The Page of Swords* and *Breath In A Ram's Horn*, on the Summit Label. His poems have appeared in *New Directions #37, First Intensity, Cafe Review, Pequod, Ironwood, IKON, Prairie Schooner, Mulch,* and *Contact II.* Pines was a featured poet at the Tucson Poetry Festival in 2004, and at the 4th Annual Latin American Poetry Festival in El Salvador in October, 2005.He presently lives in Glens Falls, NY, with his wife, Carol, and daughter, Charlotte where he practices as a psychotherapist at Glens Falls Hospital, and hosts the annual Lake George Jazz Weekend.

**WAYNE ATHERTON** is senior editor of The Café Review, an award winning poetry & art journal published out of Portland, Maine since 1989. His poetry and artwork has been published in many reputable journals, on paper and on the internet.

MEMBER OF SCABRINI GROUP

Québec, Canada
2007